DOUBLE PORTRAIT

THE BARNARD WOMEN POETS PRIZE

Edited by Saskia Hamilton

2003

Figment by Rebecca Wolff

CHOSEN BY EAVAN BOLAND AND CLAUDIA RANKINE

2004

The Return Message by Tessa Rumsey

CHOSEN BY JORIE GRAHAM

2005

Orient Point by Julie Sheehan

CHOSEN BY LINDA GREGG

2006

Dance Dance Revolution by Cathy Park Hong

CHOSEN BY ADRIENNE RICH

2007

Woman Reading to the Sea by Lisa Williams

CHOSEN BY JOYCE CAROL OATES

2009

I Was the Jukebox by Sandra Beasley

CHOSEN BY JOY HARJO

2011

Our Lady of the Ruins by Traci Brimhall

CHOSEN BY CAROLYN FORCHÉ

2013

The Wilderness by Sandra Lim

CHOSEN BY LOUISE GLÜCK

2016

Double Portrait by Brittany Perham

CHOSEN BY CLAUDIA RANKINE

BARNARD WOMEN POETS PRIZE CITATION

by Claudia Rankine

Double Portrait, by turns playful, mournful, indulgent, musical, insightful, and all the way human, comes clean about our most driving desires. In the tradition of love poems to the beloved or the parent or the world, Brittany Perham takes exuberance to the forms that complement it. Here repetition, rhyme, and anaphora serve to replicate the intricacies of overwhelming feeling. This is the world before exhaustion and cynicism overtakes the lyric. Imaginative and familiar, the result is full of humor that is both rueful and sensual.

ALSO BY BRITTANY PERHAM

The Curiosities

The Night Could Go in Either Direction
(with Kim Addonizio)

DOUBLE PORTRAIT

poems

BRITTANY PERHAM

W. W. NORTON & COMPANY
Independent Publishers Since 1923
New York | London

Printed in the United States of America
First Edition

For information about permission to reproduce selections from this
book, write to Permissions, W. W. Norton & Company, Inc.,
500 Fifth Avenue, New York, NY 10110

For information about special discounts for bulk purchases,
please contact W. W. Norton Special Sales at
specialsales@wwnorton.com or 800-233-4830

Manufacturing by Berryville Graphics
Book design by Chris Welch
Production manager: Lauren Abbate

ISBN 978-0-393-35401-0

W. W. Norton & Company, Inc.
500 Fifth Avenue, New York, N.Y. 10110
www.wwnorton.com

W. W. Norton & Company Ltd.
15 Carlisle Street, London W1D 3BS

1 2 3 4 5 6 7 8 9 0

DOUBLE PORTRAITS IN FOUR SERIES

FIRST SERIES

SECOND SERIES

THIRD SERIES

FOURTH SERIES

A Note to the Reader

Each Double Portrait appears with an archival number, which serves to catalog the poem in a series. While the book presents one possible order for each series, that order is neither linear nor fixed. Imagine, instead, that the Double Portraits in each series could be viewed together in one room of a gallery. The way you proceed through each room is up to you, and may change each time you enter.

FIRST SERIES

Today I am not vomiting blood.
Tomorrow I could be vomiting blood.

It can happen after a swordfight or a sound night's sleep:
you make coffee and boom you're vomiting blood.

You don't need a doctor
to tell you it's bad news to be vomiting blood.

I've seen all the second-to-last-scenes
in which the villain or tragic hero is vomiting blood.

It doesn't matter how I feel, or felt,
about someone once he's vomiting blood.

This is how I know the villain and the tragic hero
are the same man: he's the one vomiting blood.

Tonight with my warm feelings I try to keep him alive
thinking, from far away, *no more vomiting blood.*

It's time to say I love you and mean it
to the man who's vomiting blood.

Now I'm afraid it's almost over I'm afraid.
Who stays living for long after vomiting blood?

I love you: I mean it. A daughter should
be holding the bin to catch your vomit and your blood.

DP.f.11

for Robert Perham

Sometime in the night there was only one of us.
I thought it happened when I heard the girl-voice in the street.
A late-night song like a morning song.
oh da oh da so-do da
It went along under the window a few bars then it was quiet.
Bar-closing sounds can sound a lot like that, oh oh.
Like that you might be dead but I wasn't sure.
After that the street was quiet, unusually so.

Was this when it happened? Unusually or usually?
oh da oh da oh-da da
The girl-voice was a bottle and an opener, oh da.
The girl-voice was a welcome committee, a daughter; that's what I hoped.
Tomorrow the girl-voice would be carrying you over
a sack of leafy greens and a lemon soda.

DP.f.00

Every year, in various states, I get off the plane and look for my mother.
On the other side of the security door, already waiting, is my mother.

She's the kind of person who Windexes the table directly after dinner.
I'm the kind of person who leaves the dinner plates dirty; I am nothing like my mother.

In her house, while I do my very best to be neat, she washes my clothes.
In my house, because I can't be very neat for very long, I long for my mother.

In her house, so that I will sleep more easily, she makes my bed with her electric
  blanket.
I sleep more easily because somewhere awake in the house is my mother.

In my house, in order to sleep more easily, I sing a few lullabies.
For this to work, I have to sing with the precise intonation of my mother.

She can paint a portrait in oils and fix dinner from a can of mushroom soup.
She can fix the dishwasher's plugged drain and go for days without calling her mother.

I can stay in bed for days without showering; I wear my bathing suit as underwear.
What I cannot do is go for one day without calling my mother.

On the phone, I'm likely to be grumpy, argumentative, dull, or silent.
She'll often say, cheerfully, "Life sucks then you die—take it from your mother."

We have this one thing in common: I think about myself almost all the time.
She, too, thinks about me almost all the time, she says, "because I'm your mother.

When you have a kid, you'll understand; when are you having a kid?"
For the reasons above, I think it's better I never be anyone's mother.

I know I'd better die before she does, but she says no, she'll never let this happen.
I still somehow believe that the greatest power in the universe is my mother.

When she's mildly annoyed, or when I've been away for a long time, she calls me
by my full name, Brittany Titania, which is the way of every mother.

There are certain words you can never say too many times, especially when crying:
mommy, mama, mummy, mom; where is my mother; I want my mother.

To bed without finishing the farmyard puzzle mother said
Tomorrow father said lights off I didn't fall asleep thinking of duck & chicken
Yellow & white quack & cluck beak & beak poor chicken-piece & duck-
Hole duck-piece & chicken-hole neither had made their satisfying sound
The cow had mooed the sheep had baaed over the skylight mother said
Bird tweet father said bat squeak & the duck & the chicken
Couldn't sleep being out of the farmyard barn in the dark

DP.f.12

When you're dad-close
I can smell your liver

You build the house
From the inside out

Standing on the airy platform
With a nail in your dad-teeth

Hammer hammer
It's working isn't it

I'll make a telephone
With bean cans & string

Hammer hello-o
Your dad-eye watery close

To the first wall's last nail
It's as far down to the ground

As I've ever seen
Without a railing

& when you're dad-close
I'll stay with you girl-close

I'll girl-stay without falling failing until
You're on the ground or in it

Everyone's writing poems for the dead,
those who have gone
missing, those who have gone.
Everyone's writing poems for the dead

even without meaning to, even unwillingly
we crack the brain's back door
for children, for lovers, who set their door
swinging, who come back, even unwillingly,

to tell us something we think we hear
in her singular smoker's voice,
when lately we believed in no voice
but our own. We think we hear

her beside us in the kitchen
lifting our hair—see how we've brought
her home! see how she's brought
her cigarette. We breathe in. The kitchen

after this is predictably dark.
Already the visitation is a memory,
already we suspect *visitation* is only memory
lighting the film in the chamber's dark.

It’s certainly a flash in our particular brain
that captures our particular other,
her hippocampal Polaroid exposed, no other
way to certainly find her. Our painbrain

recalled her, momentarily, exactly.
For a second she was more ours
than she ever really was, entirely ours.
We go on recalling her consciously, inexactly,

to keep her from going again, she who was
(we’d like to believe it) telling us to say
what we came to say:
Don’t go, you who’ve gone. You, who were.

SECOND SERIES

All those times I said "forever"
as in, "Will you love me forever?"

then waited for you to say,
"Yes, I will love you forever,"

while you drained your glass and said
instead, "There is no forever,"

if in a bad mood or, if good,
"You'll be asking me about forever forever"

(grammatically suggesting, "until we die,"
the happy equivalent of forever),

I swiveled my stool, I drank my wine,
I knew I'd be doing this forever

come hell or high water,
come a future minus you or forever,

and it began to snow on the football fields
on the TV screens, forever

a comfort in the comforting bars
that have been around forever,

playing fields for every lover
whose question about forever

her lover can never answer
even if he tries forever,

even if he tells her, in his own words,
the perfect line ending in "forever,"

because the question she's asking
she's asking herself: "Will I love you forever?"

I drain my glass.
The answer could be yes.

DP.b.20

We woke up with you in our bed
Church bells ringing like there'd been a morning wedding

We woke up with you in our bed I wanted
Dark back and sleep so I covered my eyes with your hair

The corner church bells ringing for a weekend wedding
I covered my eyes and slept

A little more slept the toss of foggy light
I held your ass against my hips with his hips he held me

And when you were gone I smelled the pillow
For your hair your hair for my eyes

It's a while since I've held a pillow against my nose
Breathing in the smell of someone's hair

And how else to be happy
But to see how I might change my life

Fucking someone new you or choosing not to
Stripping off and laundering the bedding

We woke up next without you no weekday wedding
No bells held each other held slept a little more

DP.b.00

What I believed was true is true
I'm not right if I'm not with you

You're out tonight with another lover
And oh lover it's getting later

I know how you feel you're in the spin
What's eleven or twelve in the presence of gin

I know how it is I've been there too
One more drink and I'd be through

Looking at her and thinking of home
Where you were still awake alone

I know what it's like it's strange out there
You're close enough to touch her hair

When I'm home alone it's easy to think
You're punishing me for my too-many drinks

For touching her hair and seeing her off
And feeling as though I couldn't have stopped

But I know what it is this feeling you're feeling
It's hard and harder to keep your bearing

Do you get in the cab with her
Or come to our bed and have it be over

If you're wanting both simultaneously
As you're taking the subway home to me

I know how you feel I know how you feel
We both agreed on the verb to feel

Come home the light will be on
The light will be on as you have done

As you have been I'll be awake
I'll tell you there was no mistake

What we believe is true is true
You're seeing me through I'm seeing you through

DP.b.21

I want to kiss you now I want to kiss you
then I want to kiss you again I want to kiss you
when your mouth is full of chocolate
& when your mouth is full of wine &
though your mouth is not always mine
for kissing I want to kiss you I want to
kiss you in the morning before you've eaten
one sweet bite of the apple left by the bed
in the French tradition I want to kiss you
when at night you set the apple very red
by the bed I want to kiss you & in bed
when you say this is the French tradition
of lovers I want to kiss you though I'm skeptical
I want to kiss you & when you say I want to kiss you
I want to kiss you more & while I'm kissing you
I want to kiss you again & again I'm sad
while kissing you nearly weeping
while kissing you you're so close
to leaving & when you're gone I kiss you
in memory & even now kissing you gone
gone even now kiss even now I'm kissing you

I miss you meteorically metaphorically
I miss you merrily missing you
makes me mistake other women on the street
for you missing you I miss
my train I miss your train when missing you
I miss the exit ramp I miss you
& there's an empty wine glass
in my chest & my chest thinks it's missing
organs so I miss my heart I miss the way
it feels to have a stomach I miss you mornings
afternoons nights missing you sucks
away the day missing you I mis-teach meter
rhyme how to scan a line missing you like
there's no tomorrow there's no tomorrow
in which I do not miss you missing you
makes me sweaty makes me mad is maddening
I miss you & mis-punctuate or don't miss missing
punctuation altogether I miss you
murderously I miss you mountainously
metaphorically & actually I miss you most
minutes before you even leave I'm missing you

I want to kill you when I wake up
I want to kill you all day & after I kill you
I want to nap & wake up killing you
again when you're leaving I want to kill you
when you leave after kissing me
I want to kill you especially
after kissing so good I want to kill you
with hacksaw with chainsaw with each cliché
blade I want to kill you by opening
each time-release pill & releasing
their trueblue granules into your soda
killing you through bendable straw
killing you with these little hands with my toes
in your nose my underwear in your mouth
I want to invent new ways to kill you who
needs a hacksaw a chainsaw I'll kill you
by communicating with God I'll kill you
by believing in God if I have to I'll kill you off
in my dreams even if it means I have to kill off
sleep I'll kill you & keep you from leaving
& kissing-&-leaving & leaving myself I'll kill you

I want to keep you from harm keep you
from crying I want to keep you confined
to the bed I want to keep you
by keeping you close I want to keep you close
to orgasm I want to keep you coming
back I want to keep your pectorals & shins
your middle-of-the-night thing for Wheat Thins
& omelets I want to keep you cooking
especially your pasta sauce I want to keep it
in Tupperware in the freezer I want it to keep
forever I want to keep kissing you I want to
keep wanting you I want to keep you wanting
I'll keep you drugged if I have to
I'll keep you company I promise I'll keep
time with a tambourine to your trombone
keep you cool in the summer keep fanning you
with books I'll keep warm in the winter
with your breath in my hands
I want to keep your breath in your chest
for longer than my breath will keep
I want to keep you kept

You be Writer   I'll be Wife
Call me Wifelet   Wolflet
(Do you love me in a hairnet?)
The-only-she Smurfette
Pirouette   SafetyNet
(Is it time for children yet?)
Breadmaker   Bedmaker   SouthernDrawlDoll
Baker   Nametaker   PrizeDinnerDate
(I've never once been late.)
Darling   Darlette
Baby, aren't you wet yet?
Typist   Typecast   MrsYou
(How would a blow-up woman do?)
You're the Writer   Here's Your Wife

I leave my bowl in the sink
till you wash it you do it
so loudly it wakes me
up nasty you make
the coffee I drink it I'm a little
more with it so I make the bed
I'd like to be praised
you'd like some help
with the dish rack it's molding
I'd buy a new one
but this one you say
will end up in a landfill
or worse in the trash swirl
that's gathering off
our very own coast
who cares
it's too late
there's no water in California
we'll live in a desert
but I hate deserts they're dry
it's unnatural to see
how far you can see
& if you cared about water you'd stop
washing the dish rack I'll buy one

I read your new book
it's great now I'm sulky
I get a new job
insurance!
it's great now you're sulky
but also you're happy I'm happy
I'm happy you're happy
It's payday
I buy some champagne
you cook some shellfish
I drink so much
I'm starting to think
I've got the new book
you've got the new job
we're rich
we're successful
we're—
I get misty & bitchy
pick a fight about napkins
who needs them
we've got paper towels
no need to wash them
it's classic you say
the night ending this way

You say sorry all morning
I say sorry all morning
hungover I'm older
than last night
you go to Safeway
to buy chocolate ice cream
my favorite in sundaes
I eat the whole pint
with sprinkles & cherries
leave my bowl in the sink
till you wash it you do it

We lay there after for not very long
Got later got evening
With my two thumbs I opened her
Got darker got serious
She let me look as one who has been looked at
Can stand to be looked at can like it
As one who is comfortable
She lay there calmly without effort
It took all my effort
I who have never been comfortable
I who have lain everywhere with effort
I who have done nothing calmly
Got serious got scared
Comforting would it be
Were there birds at a feeding plate
Birds of a Lovepoem it would almost seem right
Got to eating displaying
Their scared birdy frenzy
If real or if symbol it almost seems right
I looked at the one who was glad to be looked at
Until I imagined I could be comfortable
As in able to be comforted
And so could imagine also cymbals and birds
And calmly displaying a frenzy

With my two thumbs I closed her
Got darker got nighttime
And like it had taken no serious effort
We lay there after for not very long

DP.b.11

We were lovers in Phoenix. We were lovers in Houston.
We were lovers in cheap and expensive hotel rooms.

We were lovers in private. We were lovers in secret.
We were lovers in public, on porch swings and carpet.

We went to the sideshows. We went to the sex fair.
You pulled me over by yanking my hair.

You bought the stockings. I bought perfume.
We fishnetted our way through each afternoon.

I preferred white and you preferred red.
We both liked tequila last before bed.

We argued at breakfasts. We argued on drives.
We argued in front of our friends and their wives.

We argued at teatime. We argued at dinner.
Neither of us could determine the winner.

I packed a bag. You broke glass in my shoe.
The last thing we said was fuck you, fuck you.

But you came back when I called. I came for you.
Who would be leaving when next we were through?

DP.b.12

There's no use putting on perfume
for a Skype conversation.
It's easy to be clear about
which parts of me you'll see.

For a Skype conversation:
earrings to catch the nighttime light
so the parts of me you'll see
will be sparkly and well-lit.

(A ring would catch the nighttime light.)
You'll appear on-screen;
you'll be sparkly and well-lit,
wearing your paw-print pajamas.

You'll appear on-screen
in a familiar corporate hotel,
wearing your paw-print pajamas,
drinking room-service wine.

In familiar corporate hotels,
we'll have to begin to talk, when
drinking room-service wine
and fucking is what we do best.

We'll have to begin to talk, when
it's hard to know what's coming next,
when fucking is what we do best
and what I want is to lie with you.

It's hard to know what's coming next:
who can say if we'll be together
when what I want is to lie with you
whether or not either of us is lying

(who can say if we're in this together?)
sometimes with someone else.
Whether or not either of us is lying,
everything is true on-screen.

Sometimes with someone else
I wake up to coffee and the paper.
Everything is true on-screen,
some things off-screen too.

I'll wake up to coffee and the paper
without you in the morning.
It's easy to be clear about
which parts of me you'll see.

DP.b.14

You are my personal Twitter.
Everything's meant for you,
my single large following.
Every text or tap, every language trap.
I've walked so far

down your street,
I might as well keep walking.
How much can I say before I get to the end?
I swing the loaf of bread.
This film isn't French

isn't film.
It's French fly season.
Above your bowl, the swarm.
Above your bowl, I'm warm.
I've sung so far down your throat
my mind's well—

Keep singing!
Was everything worth it, up till now?
Can I account for my comma? My !
A comma mistake: everyone's making it.
I come in and take

        your apple, nipple.
Stand closer. We know not to
waste a single space but neither of us is sure
about all the breaks—how much
does this count?

        We eat up
the hour lie down liecloser nearly time
for me to be leaving. Our pastpastime.
An hour lie between our you&me:
it's only you & me.

DP.b.22

Today my heart said *you*
I want to be with you above all others
though not very long
ago my heart said *her*
I want to be with her more
than I'll ever want to be with anyone else
& because I couldn't
go on living without her
not for another minute
I began living with her & all this
time I was happy I was happy
to be happy I believed
things would continue
this way every day always
but today all day
& on & on through
the night all night with my head
on her chest my heart said
though I said *no no* my heart
said & would not stop saying
you you yes you

I try to want it but I don't.
When serving lunch, you give me the better sandwich.
This is something I'll never have to question.
We eat in perfect silence.

When serving lunch, you give me the better sandwich;
you pour the water and the coffee.
We eat in perfect silence.
We can sit together all afternoon looking at the snow.

You pour the water and the coffee.
You are deep inside your head.
We can sit together all afternoon looking at the snow
not knowing how long ago we came or when we'll go.

I am deep inside my head.
The house is only borrowed so it's content
not knowing how long ago we came or when we'll go.
Someday I'd like to get inside your head and dig around.

The house is only borrowed so we're content.
There won't be time to plant a garden.
Someday I'd like to get inside your head and dig around.
Some days you'd like to wake up somewhere else.

There won't be time to plant a garden.
I try to want it but I don't.
Some days I'd like to wake up somewhere else.
This is something I'll never have to question.

There won't be time to plant a garden.
I call for you when I wake up. You don't answer.
Some days I'd like to wake up somewhere else
but not today. I put on my glasses.

I call for you when I sit up. You don't answer
the way you always do, every day
but not today. I put on my galoshes.
I find you shoveling the walk

the way you always do, every day
after a big snow.
I find you shoveling the walk,
the negative of a snowman

after a big snow
in your round black coat.
Like a Christmas-movie snowman,
you do a funny dance.

I wear your round brown coat.
I take the second shovel.
You do a funny dance.
What can I do when you've done everything?

I take the second shovel,
I dig around a shrub.
What can I do when you've done everything?
We horse-breathe beside the fence.

I kick around a shrub.
I want you to warm my fingers with your breath.
We horse-breathe beside the fence:
there's nothing left to do.

You warm your fingers with your breath.
I want to make you sandwiches and coffee.
There's nothing left to do.
There won't be time to plant a garden.

There's nothing left to do.
No matter what I'm wanting
(and wanting is a tricky thing)
I want to sit down to sandwiches and coffee.

No matter what I'm wanting,
I'm glad to find you somewhere in the house.
I want to sit down to sandwiches and coffee.
I want the icicles longer on the gutter.

I'm glad to find you somewhere in the house
doing your after-work doings.
I want the icicles longer on the gutter.
I hope for white bread, radishes, and butter.

Doing your after-work doings,
you're as happy as you ever seem.
I hope for white bread, radishes, and butter.
I want you to call me lover.

You're as happy as you ever seem.
You pour the coffee then the cream.
I want you to call me lover.
I want you to kiss me on the cheek.

You pour the coffee then the cream.
When we stir we might be the same person.
From whose lips the kiss on whose cheek?
Wanting is a tricky thing.

DP.b.15

I don't know why it seems important to tell you now that it wasn't a hickey
you saw on my neck in the exact clichéd hickey-
location under the ear where hickeys have been hickeyed since the first hickey
when what you said was *you have a hickey*
& what you meant was *from another lover* & you couldn't stand it not the hickey
or the other lover & yes it could've been another lover's hickey
but it wasn't in this case just a hickey-
looking patch of peeling skin problematic as a real hickey
I don't know why it seems important to bring up a little thing like a hickey
or why I want to tell you that my last hickey
was weeks before on my thigh & from you except that I know whatever hickey
you're giving your new woman now you'll get a kick out of knowing this hickey
story our last story let's call it The Fight of the Non-Hickey
Hickey That Sucked in Everything.

On my birthday you gave me a fistful of tissue roses,
tattoo-blue and wired together into a single green stem.
You carried them up to the roof-deck bar.
We kissed in the bathroom line beneath a wedding-white tent.
It was uncharacteristically sunny. I was twenty.

Twenty-two, and the roses are no longer blue.
I keep them in a jar on the desk where if there's sun, there's sun.
I smell the inside of the bleaching urchin for sea.
I listen inside the spiral shell for sea. Then I look out at the alfalfa.
I was twenty when I knew you, and twenty-one.

Twenty-two and I was not expecting to write this so soon,
which must mean I was expecting to write it.
Is that any way to say I do? Who starts out at the end
and still starts out? You'd say it was a problem of boundaries.
We loved, at one time,

to throw that word around. I still can't hold
the definition in my head, as with "rubric" or "prodigal."
There are a few other things I can't quite get a fix on.
The placement of the period: inside or outside the quotation mark?
If there is no rhyme, and no meter, how do you find the boundary

of the line? It seems now that every line should end with "you"
because this would best mimic the working of my brain.
But the method is impractical.
I'm not writing a ghazal. I can't give you that kind of space.
If I die first, will you still be the one to burn my drafts?

I'm not sure now if this is the kind of contract that because of its seriousness
(and because I'm dead) outlasts all other contracts,
like the one in which we agree not to know each other.
There are two contingent problems: How will you get the house key?
How will you know I'm dead?

It could be years have passed. I finally left this shithole and you
left this shithole long ago. I didn't leave you
a forwarding address. When last I saw you
you said you were moving West. Isn't that a perfect end? you
said. I hope it isn't true. I'll miss you.

Years ago when the men left the women
or the lover left or was left by her lover
and one of them boarded the White-Sailed Ship
bound for one promising continent or the other
there was no global cell phone to power up on her arrival
and no e-mail not even Internet in the Tropical Paradise
which had grand furnishings and dark rum and pioneer-type men
while the other who was not in this paradise
sat down at her desk under a London-Gray
or CambridgeMassachusettsInWinter-Gray window
on which it was raining and dashed off a letter
and bound it with string and sealed it with wax
and bundled it aboard the Very Next White-Sailed Ship
bound for the correct continent and months passed
and months passed until she had to wonder
a) did the ship with her letter go down?
b) did the ship with her lover go down?
c) did her lover find another pioneering lover whose ship had come in?
and she paced and pined and paced until her slippers wore out
and then she climbed to the top of the house
where she battled the treachery of wind through a trapdoor
to get out on the widow's walk
where at least she could see the ocean
and spit on it and slosh her whiskey over it and howl at the moon
or in a more hopeful moment think "same moon!"
and after all this she expected her lover's letter and her lover

less and less though there were still some days
too many days when she thought she was dying
for the appearance of a bright white sail
that had never been sent by a lover she'd never see again.
But she didn't die. She got older.
She arrived at a moral. Always the story is the same.
The men leave the women and the women leave the women
though this year a cell phone will work anywhere and everywhere
has Wi-Fi especially the Promising Pioneering Paradise
which has grand furnishings dark rum an infinity pool and you.
And always the questions are the same too:
Are you reading this? Will you be writing back?

THIRD SERIES

_____ people _____ people _____ people are people

restaurants should hire _____ people for the front of the house and _____ people for the back of the house restaurants do not have a history of hiring _____ people for the front of the house and _____ people for the back of the house

Apple should hire _____ people Google should hire _____ people Facebook should hire _____ people

how much do _____ people know how much do _____ people know?

law firms should hire _____ people salons should hire _____ people universities should hire _____ people law firms salons universities do not have a history of equally hiring _____ people

no place has a history of equally hiring _____ people what if many places most places all places hired _____ people yes all places!

in this land _____ people do not have jobs what if _____ people wanting jobs could get jobs yes _____ people _____ people _____ people!

_____ people use language _____ people!

_____ people give their children certain languages _____ people give their children uncertain languages too

____ people have received language certain and uncertain

certain gifts are especially risky but what other gifts do ____ people have?

____ people use language to construct certain phrases

____ people is a risky phrase to risk constructing

to begin a sentence with the phrase ____ people is riskier still

____ people use language to construct certain phrases to begin certain grammatical sentences

____ people use certain adj. + noun phrases to begin certain grammatical sentences

in this land ____ people may use certain adj. + noun phrases and ____ people are allowed to follow certain adj. + noun phrases with any combination of verb adverb prepositional phrase direct object indirect object in order to make certain grammatical sentences

this is not true for ____ people at all times or for ____ people at this time

this is not true for ____ people in all lands or for ____ people in this land

in this land ____ people may follow certain adj. + noun phrases with any combination of verb prepositional phrase direct object indirect object to make certain grammatical generalizations but for ____ people this is a risky matter

generalization about ____ people is a risky matter

generalization by ____ people is an especially risky matter

there are consequences for ____ people yes for ____ people!

to talk about this is a risky matter not to talk about this is an especially risky matter

are ____ people aware of this?

for ____ people being aware is especially complicated yes especially risky

____ people must consider their relationship to grammar for ____ people certain grammatical constructions lead to certain sentences

____ people give their children certain grammatical constructions that lead to certain sentences

certain sentences last a lifetime

_____ people have a certain responsibility to languages phrases sentences grammars generalizations _____ people have a certain history with languages phrases sentences grammars generalizations and for _____ people this is especially complicated

for _____ people responsibility is especially complicated yes for _____ people

taking responsibility might be the most important task for _____ people in this land at this time in all lands at all times

how do you see yourself fitting into the phrase _____ people how do you see me fitting into the phrase _____ people how do I see myself fitting into the phrase _____ people?

_____ people fill in the phrase in certain and uncertain ways

_____ people are doing it now

_____ people have a responsibility

for _____ people filling in and following this phrase with a sentence is especially complicated yes especially complicated

the sentence following will be a sentencing of children of _____ people a sentencing of _____ people in all lands at all times

yes a long sentence in all lands at all times we are about to begin

The Cathedral

like every day
in America
which is to say

in the Cathedral

tragedy should be
individual
un-in-common
this is normal

in the Cathedral

radios collectively
uncollect us
in commute cars
this is what we expect
a sun-and-blue day

speaking in the Cathedral

a single white bud
on a single white wire
in a single ear

speaking soon in the Cathedral

this is what we want
engines idle
windows open
isn't it spring everywhere

in the Cathedral

some of us wipe coffee

from car seats
some of us

                                    will be speaking soon in the Cathedral

have little
children
isn't it Monday
everywhere still
couldn't it have been

                                    he will be speaking soon in the Cathedral

a firework a salute
weren't there banners
runners
oh how long

                                    our president will be speaking from the Cathedral

until the end
of the morning

                                    we take you now to the Cathedral

how long
will we look like this
celebrating

                                    the president speaking now from the Cathedral

rush hour
rush hours
has the pattern changed?

9,885,998 of us watched the clip of a hatching duckling
One of us went to podcasts
One of us heard the voices of old men and knew poetry was there
One of us was male, male
One of us went to dramas, hoopskirts, and carriages
One of us heard the voices of old men and knew poetry was elsewhere
One of us binged
One of us posted a pic of a lean-to with a white person inside
One of us posted trap
One of us felt trap
One of us performance
One of us posted nothing
One of us performed poet
One of us was told to occupy, ossify
One of us lived in an A-frame
One of us framed artwork
One of us was occupied
One of us considered the terms tipi, wigwam, chum, lean-to, A-frame
One of us considered the letter A
One of us considered the letter Island
One of us was framed
One of us I
One of us land
One of us considered the terms of qualification
One of us requested paperwork
One of us failed to qualify

One of us failed to affix proper postage
One of us trump
One of us card
One of us trick
One of us posted a kitten trick pic
One of us was assaulted for doing nothing
One of us was accosted for saying something
One of us tagged
One of us sidestepped, skirted
One of us qualified
One of us A.C.
One of us was male, female
One of us searched the proper sites for the proper information
One of us saw the improper sights and knew the proper information
We knew
One of us drove
One of us drove down
One of us downtown
One of us twerked in the comfort of an owned home
One of us rented
One of us tripped, tipped
One of us vilified
One of us petitioned
One of us signed
One of us would never resign despite the video evidence
One of us was a visionary

One of us videoed the breading of an onion ring
One of us videoed the breading of an onion ring stuffed with cheese
One of us videoed the breaking
One of us frying
One of us the voice breaking
One of us was the choke
One of us watched
We watched
One of us was a revisionary
One of us rented out
One of us boarded the Google bus
One of us felt holier-than-
One of us was female, male
One of us was comfortable with gentrification
One of us was comfortable with the word gentrification
One of us was of a certain generation
One of us tampered, tamponed
One of us was told to prove it
One of us used the toilet
One of us loitered
One of us was boarded
One of us boarded up
One of us boxcars, boxcars, boxcars
One of us was female, female

FOURTH SERIES

DP.agp.10

first thing's
first we lose the ability to communicate
a lot of silence on the phone
yesterday I could have
figure out how to reach you
yesterday's I walks the bridge and crosses to the island
without worrying
yesterday's
I land its rocky coast

to communicate requires the ability to say what we mean even if

I could have gone back
you washing at the sink
you know I would have changed things for a while

today I wouldn't dare the bridge alone
would with no hesitation

—off the passing cars

—off the railing

—cross each painted line

you knew I
then after a while
didn't

parked islandside we got out
to stretch
the first summer out
beneath the trees a shoe
of pine needles a bed that summer a cottage
we moved into

then everything was after the first summer everything's after

DP.agp.11

The likelihood I'll talk to you
today is very small.
I'll shut in. My mind will loop
some pictures on the wall.

Today is very small:
a matchbook with an open flap,
a picture on the wall,
a postage stamp, a pocket map.

A matchbook with an open flap
won't bring back the bar,
nor the postcard stamp and pocket map
we bought. We got that far:

the back of the day-lit bar,
the third round of G&Ts.
You bought. We got that far-
away look, two divers in a sea.

The third round of G&Ts;
a few mean words.
Look away. Two divers in a sea,
no lamp or tether cords.

A few mean words:
the writing on the wall.
No lamp or tether cords.
Today is very small.

I asked miracles of my body.
Where I peeled nail-thin strips from its fingers

it provided. The miracle of skin, said my body.
If we'd had a tail, I'd have chopped it off.

We don't have a tail, said my body
gratefully. Instead I had to make other cuts.

We got used to things. My body
wanted to hide behind the refrigerator door

but I summoned it. Lazy Body,
make the bed, I said. There was wine around the mouth.

I made this decree: Body,
you will feel only pain. Then I let it lie down

for the occasional Deluxe Full-Body
Massage, so it wouldn't get really discouraged.

I said, This is for you, Body,
don't you like it? But it spasmed uncomfortably

on the table. It dreamed of other things. A full-body
orgasm spasm, for example. Wine around the mouth.

Certain things I liked gave my body
no pleasure, like the sound of "orgasm spasm" aloud.

I said, Listen up, Body.
It listened. "If I worship one thing more than another

it shall be the spread of my own body,"
I read to a classroom of students

when I hated it most for its bodyish body
especially its armpit sweat.

Whitman, I hoped, might speak to my body
where I could not, because around this time

I began to worry. My body
was red around the mouth and alarming.

Breast cancer? Ulcer? Cirrhosis of the liver? Body
dysmorphic disorder? Reflux?

I dragged it from bed and let my body
see itself in the full-length mirror.

I tried saying soothing things to the fleshiest body
parts such as: I love you, breasts. I love you, stomach.

Don’t you believe me, Body?
But neither of us believed me.

We need a miracle, I said to my body.
But it wasn’t up for any miracle-making.

Stop feeling pain! I commanded. . . . Body?
But it was the only thing either of us knew how to feel.

DP.agp.12

I have to stop it so I will.
Climb over the hill.
Blow into town like a small fog.
Walk directly beside the frogs
and crickets. Scatter
the buzz with an engine.
Pick at the tips of 10-cent corn.
Black teeth in a sunny mouth a bottle of gin.
Win at Bingo! Win at trivia!
Win a two-for-one sail on the Riviera.
This isn't a Riviera this is a real boat.
Hey. Pull the lines, start the winch.
The trap comes up inch by inch.
Too square for a body.
Too short for that sort of box.
The man beside me's at a loss.
He's got a story about a rope
caught easy around an ankle
he's hoping not to tell me.
What do you call that knot?
He's looking into the water.

DP.agp.13

I'm lying on the mat, won't someone bring me a piña colada?
In winter I buttoned you into the hood of your parka.
The sun hits me in the third eye.
It wouldn't blow off even in the snowstorm.
This is the meditation portion of today's video.
Just a few wet curls.
I tried a hair tonic to turn me into a prince.
In spring you buttoned yourself into a hood of silence.

The sun gives me a tracheotomy.
I do this part without the teacher.
Sternum, navel, lower but no orgasm, gone behind a building.
Pretty soon the music and the credits.
So many split ends!
You wouldn't hear me through the PrimaLoft even if I wanted you to.

DP.agp.31

I stand at the podium
praising him.

I'm pink and casual. I look
at the audience: anywhere-but-him.

I tried on my dresses
speaking to him:

It's nice to see you,
I tried on telling him.

Go for a drink?
I tried on asking him.

Then I practiced my undressing,
just in case, in front of him.

Take off your shirt?
Tonight I'll ask him.

Take off your pants.
He'll want me to tell him.

I stand at the podium
praising him.

I conclude my smartest remarks.
Everyone claps for him.

He kisses my cheek and forgets my name.
I don't want to embarrass him.

DP.agp.32

for Kirstin Valdez Quade

I don't need to climb into bed with you.
This makes all things possible.
But I want you just as much as any "you"
I'd like to fuck, without the miscible
desire-depression cocktail. After I see you,
I go home feeling beautiful, a success!
I like how beautiful you
are. I never want to see you less
and I can want to see you
more without losing my will to live.
I can think of you from here—you
at the desk beneath the lofted bed
or in the garden with your hair undone, you
with your parrot defoliating the fig
or with the lover I love for you—
without wishing I were there instead.
I can always, day or night or three a.m., call you
up so you can chant the You-Are-Not-Alone
Chant, which goes, ad infinitum, "You-
Are-Not-Alone." If you think this isn't a love
poem, think again. This one's for you,
ad infinitum, for you.

—a sky, say, and birds to suggest loneliness.
A girl walks a street where birds don't sing or do.
It's fall, with falling leaves—

I want to believe in the birds I wrote and in the birds still written
(poetic-closure birds, a common species)

—the sky they fly is gray or heavy,
the girl beneath it gray or heavy metaphorically speaking,
and sad romantically speaking, and so literally thin—

and in the girls I wrote and was
leaving yet another bed believing birds could hold that feeling or sing it.

Bird, girl, sky: they provided me real comfort.
And yes—the sky rained
like tears—and yes I broke the line astonished with my power.

What words could provide such comfort now?
What breaks?

You are not here nor will be, my narrative entrance.
Nothing in this room will bear a symbol.
Rightly so.

We reduced our time to one museum afternoon,
our drinks to one, then one we shared in separate flutes,
a chaste geometrical cheese plate, two knives.
My wife we talked of not at all,
nor the nights I rattled your hall on the dark way to bed,
nor anything that might suggest an attitude or feeling
other than the friendliness we'd agreed on without saying.
Your earring was your earring was your earring.
The familiar un- in the bar mirror.
Ear, hair, hand, and—No and.
We grew strange strange stranger.
To make things light we made critiques of what we'd seen:
the charcoals, we thought, seemed rather black and white.
We hoped the time would never end/end soon.

DP.agp.20

for Amy Clampitt

It's hard to believe a world is out there.
I'm waiting for you to come home.
Amy says, *Many have died of it already.*
Spring could come and

I'd be waiting for you to come home.
Amy says, *A fondling session comes with the inevitable risk—*
Spring will come and
I'll be alone in this little box of a room.

Amy says, *A fondling session comes with the inevitable risk*
of being laughed at—is it habit, is it altogether voluntary?
Alone in this little box of a room,
a "fondling session" seems like everything!

(Amy's laughing.) Is it habit—it isn't altogether voluntary—
that makes me wait for you as often as I do,
that makes this cultivation seem like everything?
Such an excess of cultivation all but asks us to stop breathing,

which makes me think of you as I always do
when something smart is said. You:
such an excess then such starvation I'm almost not breathing.
It's just a walk, you said.

When something smart is said, it's you.
How long will it last? I said.
It's just a walk, you said.
I'm soft and deflated as Amy's sofa.

How long will it last? Amy says,
I thought for half a second, snow. But no.
I'm soft and deflated as Amy's snow
watering Amy's yard and Amy's grave.

I think for half a second, No. And no
spring will come.
It's hard to believe a world is out there.
Amy says, *Many have died of it already.*

Double Portrait

When will you stop being You
who fits inside my catchall Thou,
the one I post each letter to?
When will you stop being You?
A pronoun never loved or grew.
I return you to your common noun:
then will You stop being you.
Who fits inside my catchall Thou?

ACKNOWLEDGMENTS

Thanks to the editors of the following journals in which these poems appeared: *32 Poems*, *The Adroit Journal*, *The Collagist*, *The Journal*, *The Knox Writers' House*, *Southern Humanities Review*, *Southwest Review*, *Poetry Crush*, and *Poetry Daily*. Thanks to Claudia Rankine for believing in the poems. Thanks to Jill Bialosky, and everyone at Norton, for supporting this book. Thanks to Saskia Hamilton and the Women Poets Program at Barnard. Thanks to my friends and teachers in the Stanford Creative Writing Program, especially Eavan Boland, W. S. Di Piero, and Ken Fields. Thanks to my teachers at the University of Virginia. Thanks to my students everywhere. Thanks to the James Merrill House Writer-in-Residence Program. Thank you: Kim Addonizio, Deborah Digges, Charlotte Gordon, Barbara Helfgott Hyett, Dana Kletter, Randall Mann, Donna Masini, C. J. Perham, D. A. Powell, Kirstin Valdez Quade, Sarah V. Schweig, Matthew Siegel, and Lisa Russ Spaar. Thank you to Jennifer Foerster. Thank you to Leigh Perham. Thank you to Peter Kline, for all of it.